KITH

Also by the Same Author:

Jo Bell's 52 project started with a simple idea: *Write a poem a week. Start now. Keep going.* In the 52 weeks that followed, the global workshop group became a phenomenon as poets took up the challenge and thousands of poems were written and shared.

Now, for the first time, all 52 poetry-writing prompts are collected together, and you can try them for yourself to create your own year of poetry writing – no matter when, where or how you decide to start.

How to be a Poet is a twenty-first century guide to writing well by Jo Bell and Jane Commane and special guests. It combines advice, ideas and encouragement from experienced poets and editors in topical chapters to examine both the technical and creative dimensions of being a poet.

There is plenty for everyone here, and topics range from redrafting poems and getting them published, to learning to pay attention and look and listen like a poet. It encourages you to read widely, write fearlessly and actively participate in the life-changing, life-enhancing force for good that is poetry.

Find these and more poetry titles online at:

www.ninearchespress.com

KITH

Jo Bell

Nine
Arches
Press

Kith
Jo Bell

ISBN: 978-0-9931201-0-7

First published April 2015 / reprint 2018 by:

Nine Arches Press
Unit 14
Sir Frank Whittle Business Centre
Great Central Way
Rugby
CV21 3XH
United Kingdom

www.ninearchespress.com

Printed in Britain by:
ImprintDigital●●● ●●●●

Some will tell you that you are mad, and nearly all will say, 'What is the use?' For we are a nation of shopkeepers, and no shopkeeper will look at research which does not promise him a return within a year. And so you will sledge nearly alone, but those with whom you sledge will not be shopkeepers: that is worth a good deal.

– Apsley Cherry-Garrard, *The Worst Journey in the World*

About the Author:

Jo Bell is a poet, broadcaster and teacher whose poetry aims for 'an absolutely unsentimental tenderness'. Born in Sheffield and raised in Derbyshire, she lives on a narrowboat on the English canal system. Winner of the Charles Causley Prize for poetry and the Manchester Cathedral Prize, in 2015 Jo received an honorary doctorate for services to poetry. Her poetry books include *Navigation* (now available as an eBook), and two poetry handbooks, *52: Write a Poem a Week. Start Now. Keep Going* and *How to be a Poet* (Nine Arches Press). Find her @Jo_Bell and jobell.org.uk.

Contents

For my kith, with thanks:
and for the Jonathans, with apologies.

Crates

Observe that when I speak of crates
your mind supplies one straight away.

Likely you are thinking of the fruiterer's crate:
a shallow slatted box of rain-napped pine,
the archetype of apples stencilled on the side,
a cartouche slot above it for a grocer's hand.

Your crate may be the sturdy plastic tub
of the eco-minded council, waiting at the gate
with all its rinsed tomato cans
and in this case a drowned frog;

or then again the solid, beer-smooth wood
hefted by the publican
with its hungover slump of bottles
to the yard, the morning after.

Your crate exists as soon as it is thought.
Its shape is shown in speaking of it.
Now, let us speak of love.

Taken

'When a thief kisses you, count your teeth.' – Yiddish proverb

Let's just say it was complete surrender.
The wanted word is *visceral*; the usual
exchange of fluids doesn't quite compare.
He closed his eyes and tilted back his head
and he was mine, as naked as a worm.
He yielded like a sapling to the axe.

Humility is not an asset in my trade, but
such an ecstasy of loss brought out
the best in me, at last. I stripped.
His willingness unmanned me; such a glut
of giving. It was hard to take but oh,
I took it, breath for breath and blow for blow.

I got up with the sun; gobsmacked, lovestruck.
My keys were missing. All the doors were locked.

Like love

Snow falls on the year in sweeps and rushes;
smothers colour, gags the tracks,
stops the mouths of tell-tale lanes,
stuffs a fist into the downfall pipes.

Snow sneaks through the gap beneath the door,
appears unsummoned in the porch.
It lays its slippery gospel round the church,
slides panic under feet and wheels.

Snow betrays the fox and starves the wren.
It compacts to a lucid skim;
draws from deep white wells
to keep the townsfolk in a tightening pond.

It takes a while to settle, settles so short a while.
It brings the people out excited; sends them home
chilled to the bone, lonely to the bone,
more frightened than they can explain.

Lately

Running on the ridge, where every contrail
cuts me to the gladdest bone
I have to pause for breath.

The finches gossip over buds;
the sky of it gets in my eyes.
Spring's in its first grand panic,

rushing and retreating day by day,
checking itself with every gain
until, unstoppable, it bursts its bounds

and belts across the uplands,
races through the lines of hedge
and harrier; makes the land an epic *yes*.

That's how love comes. It counts no cost.
From here our words, our names
are small as houses in the valley.

The breath that rises in my throat
is speechless, clean as grass.

Shame

On Union Street, beneath a dishcloth sky
I pass a woman planted on the pavement
in a dressing gown and slippers.
She is poking at a man as if he were
a kidney on a butcher's slab.

She is twentyish and shouting;
lips hard, cheeks fat with anger.
He is bulky, pale with youth, hair spiked.
His eyes are low, his shoes are cheap
and he is taking it.

She's telling truths like throwing knives.
She hasn't had a fag yet.
Her breasts are full of sourness;
her eyes are red like his, like mine.
We will never know how to be kind.

I have not asked for this

The world is full of people
screwing at the service station,
drinking milk that's nearly fresh, and settling.

Still, this battered magnet keeps its force
and this charged cope around my shoulders
keeps me true. Your touch does this.

We know each other best at the beginning
after all. A little fear may murmur *This will pass:*
in answer comes a little strength that says

Then let it pass. But let it pass like Spring.

Cuntstruck

Third glass. My second finger touched her leg
for emphasis, as if I hadn't noticed.
And I hadn't noticed; till I felt
that sorry splinter bedding in,
thought *Jesus Christ, again?*
and it gathered up like water at a weir.

You have to ask yourself as you pretend
to listen to another wide-eyed tale,
check your wallet for a condom,
inject that bubble in your own damn vein
why at the age of forty-nine
it never ends. It never bloody ends.

Talking to myself

When he comes back from the bathroom in ten minutes
buttoning his old black Levi's, and sits
like a tired Grace in your half-sprung chair:

when he touches his dark and silver curls
bemused, and looks at you full-on
as if you were the answer to the question:

when he laughs, so that the pleasure of his laugh
is like a whetstone for your needs
his skin a scent that you'll remember like a dog

for twenty years: when you notice the spot
of blood on his sleeve: when the penny drops
like a bomb into the loading bay

do me a favour:

leave.

Enough deathbed talk:

the business of our days is whether to endure
these gobshite hours and slingshot seconds
or to praise. The season helps; a yellow beach,
Whitsunday sun on gulls and gables. Here and now

it's shallows turned to sea glass; windblown dogs
and boats in harbour, bracken tousled on the hills;
your sweat-and-solid body shifting in my sheets.
Praise paddles in with every kayak.

Sometimes it's otherwise. We wake stone-still
and cry for night to end the days as soon as they begin
and nothing stays but dirty plates, new forms
of the impossible. Scarce room then for praise.

Stay close. When the clay sticks to our hectic feet
we'll pull each other up until we're clear,
address the only business of our days:
hold strong, hold strong and hold to praise.

Fig roll

Everybody knows that poets have a lot of sex.
They tumble vividly into the beds
of friends and peers, destroying marriages
and furniture, get claret on the linen

then write it up in copperplate – obliquely,
with sufficient hints to give the editor a clue
to the identity of each and each,
and always hoping for a good review.

Muse

for the Shipwright, who did

You show up late
in your biker jacket
hoping that a quick roll
on my laminate floor
will remedy all ills.

It will:
but make it a good one.

No Seafarer

I sing my own true story, tell my travels
small as they are, of episodes on shallow channels;
working up to Wolverhampton through the Twenty One
or drifting into Diglis, gagging for a cup of tea.

It's all about me: my boat, my slow-mo marvels,
my lockside affairs – a spaniel saved from death,
a wisecrack for the fat gongoozler. That day
on the Llangollen, storm-glazed, glad together.

The overgrowing straits that carry me
from one pub to the next, the river mouths
and long-dead ferry points where knackered boats
would carry sheep across at dusk;

I sing their praises daily, bank to bank.
A narrow span, a slight adventure
of slight travels, yes. But still my own, and true
and still, for all that, sung.

Given

A dark man gave me this, and it was everything:
a cabin twelve by six, and Severn rising limitless.
No romance, no quarter; little rest.

In his coffin bunk, our skins, the channels of my wrist
were specks of engine oil and wine, small piracies of self.
We made a travellers' pact to go wherever water let us pass,
together until each stood in the other's way.

His second gift was a clean parting. Love passes,
water stays. Inconstant: always borrowed, never spent.
A better woman would be sorry now.

Springtime at the boatyard

You can keep your cuckoos. We hear Spring's first song
in the sound of angle-grinders, brazen as a mating call
across the yard; the saw blades and the welders
working between weathers like a nesting bird,
and swarf as bright as daffodils on workshop floors.

You can keep your catkins. We have rust like pollen
on our skins. We walk between steel shells, and smell
the fresh blue boiler suits of all the coming days, when warmth
will stretch our hulls and make of summer evenings
a shed for building this year's stories.

Breaker's yard

Mid-afternoon, and Billy Dog is welding patches
on the colander-bottomed boat across the yard.
Between the sparkler crackles of acetylene
I hear him wondering when I'll say yes.

Today I've made his tea in the mug that says
CONTROL FREAK. Last week he was GOD.

The cat sashays across the car park.
Billy tips his mask to get some air.
I'd better go and get that mug back,
ask him how it's going; tell him no.

Tied up

Tonight you moor at Tixall Wide beneath the giddy bats.
A heron tries one leg. The boat is tethered loosely,
browsing between bank and channel.

In dry dock once, you saw her settle on the bostocks,
wondered at her bulk; that welded self
as helpless as a brick. Her power's in suspense.

You don't need to travel far. You're always home.
There's comfort in the play of rope;
slack and tight, there and back.

Tixall Wide

Staffordshire and Worcester Canal

The cut is working water. Straightened,
straitened, boxed and sluiced; contained
and discontent. Worrying at banks,
whitening the heels of boats.

All day it's run from lock to weir, from weir
to pound. It earns its rest by evening,
dawdles through a leaking lock;
puts up a weary bubble, iris-cool.

Now it kicks off muddy boots;
a worker done with work.
It breathes out ozone, laundry-sweet
and ruffles sedge and vetch,

idly spins a swan. What it does
is not so simple as stilling the mind.

Frozen in

You wake, and know.
The boat is still as bones
and you, its red heart beating.

The canal was taken in its sleep
and paved with cold. The chilled air
gathers round your feet.

The ice, disgruntled, shifts
and chews a little on the hull,
sets itself to set again.

Beneath the glaze, fish flicker
like grey flames,
silent, watchful.

Inside, you go on with business;
making tea,
waiting for crocuses.

How
to
live
on a
narrow
boat

Walk
slowly

and
quite often
sideways.

There is
no room
for books
for vases;
sentiment.

Within
the span
of a
tall man's
arms
live

lively as
a woman's
hands:
mindful
of
one need

which can
be met
by
moving on

and
always
buoyant.

My country

takes years to find me, comes by water
in its own sweet time, doesn't mind much
if I lag or fall behind; never waits.

We meet at gravelled river bends
in clay-and-crow land, beyond words
like *Worcestershire* or *London*.

This unpromised land, this country
without self; its private happiness,
its snoozy dawdling at city-back or meadow.

We know each other just a little –
it, the thing that laid me down like silt,
and me, a momentary factor; soft-walled cell

within the leaf within the lively forest,
adding one small dot of matter
to its wood-slow happenings.

Kingfisher

The shot that starts the half-willing heart;
nano-warrior, dart. God's shuttlecock,
a blue smack on the grey day's arse.
Astonishing; across the river's drab and smudge
this bright harbinger comes fast
to tell someone they made it, that they're *in*.
The river's knuckle-duster flashes its little fist,
comes cherry-knocking at the door of dusk –
and you, open-mouthed as a fish on the hook:
no-one there when you look.

Oiks

The walk may be Churchillian, chin in and belly first.
You don't fool me. You water-Cockney mallards
with your nightclub swagger; I've seen you
fucking in the shallows, shouting like a bus-stop drunk.

You're drab and scrawny TWOCkers
cruising for an open door: on patrol
and on the ante, cocky as the Little Ships,
common as muck.

Over here lads, there's some bird with a sandwich.
Don't give us plate-scraped lettuce, couscous,
scraps of rocket for fuck's sake; we want bread
and none of your granary shit.

What do we want?
BREAD.
When do we want it?
NOW, and NOW, and NOW.

Lunchtime you're hungover, slouching on the bank
and muttering; at midnight, up for anything
and new-tattooed. That stripe of Primark colour on each wing,
the old-fashioned gang rape every spring;

She's down. Get in.

Still life

The ice is thick as bottle bottoms.
In the little villages of hedge and ditch
the birds are hungry as a needle's eye.

Even this shallow February day
will give the boats a rub of warmth
along their backs. The hulls will stretch.

The snowdrops make a break for it.
The hawthorn holds its breath
and bides its time. And so will I.

Boat in dry dock

Alive in water, dead in dock.
A welded tongue; she's fluent wet
and dumbstruck dry.

Under way, a knife; she cuts the surface,
frays the bank. Here, it's spark and sawdust,
scrape and solder, grind and burn.

Too much air. She wants a navigation,
sluices, channelled wet, the rain
to lick her ropes and scuppers.

She wants her own weight
hanging in her long black hide again,
her pitted hull, her rusts.

The cut pours in to ease her steel.
She thinks of floating; bobs and shivers,
tries herself against the flood, and

holds. The welcome shift
of everything, the balance
and the give!

Lifted

The land says – *come uphill*: and water says
I will. But take it slow.

A workman's ask and nothing fancy –
Will you? Here's an answer, engineered.

A leisurely machine, a box of oak and stone;
the mitred lock, the water's *YES*.

We're stopped. The bow bumps softly
at the bottom gate, and drifts.

All water wants, all water ever wants,
is to fall. So, we use the fall to lift us,

make of water its own tool, as simple
as a crowbar or a well-tied knot;

open up the paddles, let it dam and pucker,
lift and with it, lift us like a bride, a kite,

a wanted answer, breath no longer held
or like a boat. We're on our way

and rising. Water rushes in like fools;
these tonnages that slip across the cill,

all dirty-bottle green and gathering into
a giddy hurl then slower, slow until

it ends in glassy bulges, hints of aftermath:
a cool and thorough spending.

Wait, then, for the shudder in the gate,
the backward-drifting boat that tells you

there and here are equal, an imbalance
righted. Ask of water; *help me rise*

and water says: *I will.*

A crossing
Portishead-Sharpness

The harbour wall that cupped us like a hand
around a lighter flame is gone. We're out
and running with the tide, the tide, the *tide*
for Christ's sake with a cargo of small selves.
My boat, my Boudicca of the tomato plants
and golf umbrellas, pushing for the other side at dawn.
My grubby whippet, slender as a sight hound!
Tinker puts her rusted muscles to the test,
fights Severn like a ratter; through the Slime Road
where the currents slide across the hidden spits,
nose up in foam as if a hundred feet of water
were her usual three, and leaping glassy spinners;
throttles up, to dash between the stanchions
of white bridges thrown across her path.
My Golden Hind of red geraniums, my lively flea,
my tractor-engined slipshod craft, my ploughshare
cutting furrows to the entrance gate. We're in.
Severn turns away. The grey gate swings;
the Gloucester and Sharpness is ready,
lays a sixteen-foot glass slipper at our feet.
Tinker ties up with a tugman's hitch
and settles in the company of swans
where she belongs. It's all sweet water now.
Her skipper, missing sleep, will wake at three
and walk the towpath naked, toes as soft as crab flesh
on the earth; finding herself thirsty again,
tilting back her throat for want of salt.

Severn, from Purton

Don't take my lightness lightly. There is gravity
behind it. This slow fix, this great meander
that supplies the land's great wants,

this fluid strength is what we borrow,
what we lean against when love inhabits us.
It alters when it alteration finds, alright

and so it should. There is no ever-fixèd mark.
The bark's the thing: the dot that battles tides
and if the river lets it, makes its small unlikely win.

The archaeologist of rivers

We study the forsaken, which after all
is commonplace. We have our specialities.
Etruscan earthenware or Saxon jewellery;
each action leaves its spoor. We call this
material culture. You call it spoons.

My own field is the archaeology of water:
the ditches cut and filled, the softening wharves.
I take the measure of the footprint left
in shifting things from making-place to market place;
armaments, immigrants, bricks and food

or earthenware and jewellery, as the century requires.
The slow machine that England was
is stamped on every bulrush boatyard, on the lock gate
knocking home. I tread from sluice to mill-race,
give each one its small place in the record:

the worked stone on the bank wet as an eye,
every channel filling as I pass.

Eve naming the birds

I give him language and he looks for flint.
I've done the beasts, he says. *Your turn.*
I name them into shame, weeping for their loss.

So, the wordless world is finched and hawked,
shriked and paradised into the light we make;
the swans and dodos, gannets, grebes and rails.

He cannot see a feather till it's limed:
as if dominion were what we ought to want,
as if they ought to be ashamed of merely flying.

We shall name it into shape, he brightly says –
*be it God or anything that's naked, we shall clothe it
in a word. Now, what shall we call you?*

I think it – but unspoken, it is still my own –
Enemy. From this day forward, I know
he shall bruise my head, and I his heel.

Infallible

Outside the workshop, toddlers tumbled by.
They sent me here for beauty,
said the courtier; your children are so plain.
Giotto laughed a blacksmith's laugh.

I made them in the dark, he said.
The envoy blushed, unsealed his errand:
His Holiness commands
a sample of your work.

Indeed, said Giotto. We will talk
as soon as Pietro's roof is done.
The messenger leaned in and scowled;
the Holy Father's business is to speak for God.

Giotto snatched the scroll;
returned it with a circle,
compass-perfect in a single sweep of red.
God speaks for himself, he said.

Gloriana

I like their gifts but little, and their flattery
less. They come again, and they will come
tomorrow with their single boring question.

I am heavy with their pearls and slipshod promises.
I speak six languages, and am the only woman
they can hear in any one of them.

I speak. They scrape to listen.
In six languages I slowly say
No.

A nightingale for Gilbert White
April 5, 1768

The garden's lean, but buds and shadows fatten.
A London smoke crawls west, and cucumbers
are tortoising across the sweat-sweet dung.

A nuthatch jars and clatters in the oak;
rooks get cocky in the Selborne copse. At last
the air is quick with bee-flies, kites and larks

and April falls across the parish like stained glass;
like rest for the broken-backed. The diarist
writes one word to stand for spring – *Luscinia!*

Colour blurs along the quickened hedge
into the woodsmoke hours. The nightingale
loops speechless syllables on every thorn.
Attention, after all, is prayer. Nothing goes unseen.

Mallaig

One early morning slant with rain
a woman steps out for a first smoke on the quay
and understands that there,

between the greyscale ketch and ferry,
is a whale. There's tension in the tons of brine,
a shift of waters, wait –

an epic sigh. The blowhole clenches
and the deep blank beast turns back to sea,
toward the known; its buoyant safeties, pod and kelp.

In that drenched world are sparks of fish
and leather-bottle seals: a populace
who measure time as *now* or not at all;

who graze the mile-deep plains,
make brisk and mottled journeys
on the thousand ways between our isles.

Where are they now – wet brethren,
fat slick creatures of the sea?
Their landmarks smell of fish.

They move through larger worlds
with no idea of weather,
cigarettes, necessity.

From here on up all the paths are informal

At last. The roads run out in sorry stops: the tarmac
can't be arsed and no-one needs to come here but the bees.
Always, above the fishy knotwork of a seafront town
there's such a watershed of routes; a plain place
of no camber. All roads end in grass and you are forced
to make your bloody mind up and to choose –
or shrug off choice entirely, striking out for teatime
with nothing but a bag of sandwiches and half a clue
where anything might be. Anything is not the thing
in any case. The land holds onto megaliths
and hedgerows. Metalled roads, it knows,
are just a phase we pass through now and then.

Excavation

You think it's all gold filigree
and toothbrushes. You think
that on a hill in Wales or Worksop,
a bearded man with whisky in his flask
can shape a bump of contour lines
into a narrative. You think that we
are joining dots and beeps
to amplify a whisper from the dead.

No. We break stones with picks
and scrabble over spoil for evidence;
push earth through sieves
for tooth-and-hobnail splints.
Our nails and nerves are ragged.
We hear the dead alright. They say:
Don't ask us any more.
Write your own damned story.

Small finds

What's left of anyone is the unchosen.
If I could choose, it would be these;
a Belgian bottle opener, a demob trunk,
a ruby necklace and a wooden-handled paring knife.

And I would have a boat grave,
sleeping in my long steel shell
till excavators found me, disappointed by
my legacy of swarf and fire cement.

My archaeology will be a raggedy assemblage
of spiral wires from notebook spines,
the barrel of a plastic fountain pen split like a bone
for marrow; nothing much to show.

Silbury Hill

Your Wessex megaliths are Bronze Age marker pins.
Here and *here* were special sites for feasts
or fol-de-rol. The wide green flatlands in between
were ripe for ritual procession –

druids decked in jet-and-amber gewgaws,
shamans skipping down a monumental avenue
in beads and wolf's teeth, gathering their people
at the skirts of this, a cosmic macaroon.

Back north, our stones are frank as knuckle dusters
on each ridge. Here, they say, and here
we did what everybody did. We won the stone
and worked it; got and lived and privately made way.

We're not so rich in anything that we can let it pass us by
but still – our strongholds are a wealth of contours
and our gods have never asked
that we should bend our backs to build a hill.

Mute

The Walkden and Farnworth Band strike up
and yes, they are fat and balding, with beer-wet lips
and skin grown pale in club backrooms.

They're straight-backed in their uniforms
because their wings are furled
and then they play.

This is strong music: music turned on lathes
by men who don't lament,
who speak by fighting.

This is working music; our call to prayer,
our call to sing our ordinary story
in a fierce unasked-for jubilation.

Music made in sheds or beaten into cymbals
at the shift-end. *Jerusalem* and *Danny Boy;*
they're borrowed songs but spoken in our tongue.

A ringing out, a clocking on, a moan
of disappointment sure as klezmer.
Pit head music, punching out precisely

This is us, this is. Still here.
The spotty prophets raise their clarions.
The North is clearing its throat.

My Schiehallion

There's a Schiehallion anywhere you go. The thing is, climb it.
  – Norman MacCaig, *Landscape and I*

At the top of Margery Hill
is a lean, eroding barrow made of peat.

Under the lumpen mound, a man
who knew this hill by an older name

and had another name than ours
for the valley two miles away, where

on a Bronze Age day the peat was dug;
and had a name which we will never know

for the need to carry peat
two miles uphill for a dead man.

His tracks and woods and ways
are gone

and even his technologies look simple
from a distance.

The names and armies pass like rain
on Minninglow and Shutlingsloe,

on Bosley Cloud and Thorpe Cloud,
Shining Tor, Chrome Hill and Higger Tor,

on Win Hill and Lose Hill.
Their names and mine will pass like rain

but I am buried in them, they in me:
their soil will cling to me a little when I fall.

Waiting in Starbucks for Max

for Max, naturally

Everyone else is elsewhere.
The woman next to me is crouching in
her digital dugout, screened and safe.
The men climb inside their phones.

The boy beneath his headphones
is definitely not looking at
the girl with the thin ankles
and the January hair

who is definitely not looking at him
but I'm entirely here, in black wool
and dark leather: breathing coffee,
rolling this hour on my tongue

and definitely not looking at Max
as he wakes in a flat in Rusholme,
looking wide-eyed at a broken clock –
or better, at a man worth staying in bed for.

Sleep on, my slugabed.
The hours are thick as froth.
There's time for fine words
and bad jazz on wipe-clean sofas;

so I thank you for the chance
to pick the threads from Monday,
look it up and down for once, to say
Moment – you'll do.

Raising the roof for Kirsty

Praise your thousand days of busted knuckles,
back-ache, neck-ache, dusted wire-wool hair;
of eating cheese amongst the rubble,
reading Heaney in your wellingtons
and never a clean dress to go dancing in.

Praise the day we gathered at your door
to hoist a pine branch to the eaves, and sang,
a ruddy choir under your paint-stick baton
> *The roof is finished*
> *The roof is finished*
till we were hoarse enough for beer and flames,

drank each other to a charcoal drowse
settling in half-wrapped corners –
here a one and there a swaddled pair,
easy on the floor as hounds inside a mead hall –
stationed to sleep out the hours of thunder.

And, as water found a way between
the pitchy ridge- and roof-slates, sending
piss-thin streams to wet the flagstones by her head
praise the one (whichever one it was) who,
laughing in half-sleep, got up and put the kettle on,

began the chorus that we took up one by one;
> *The roof is leaking*
> *The roof is leaking –*
waking, placing buckets, drinking tea hungover –
and what's a song for, Kirsty, anyway,
if not to keep the roof on?

Birdsong at the Rec

I only know the ones that sound like muesli
speckling the day with goodness;

the ones that sound like rusty swings
or a musical saw, the bomb going off,
the torturer's knock at the door.

The car park birds, the layby birds
of verge and brink; these ones I know.

I like the ones that sound like schnapps
with gold leaf spinning in it.
I like the day's last blackbird

holding up its song, a candle flame
as the street lights flicker on.

Beginnings

Forgive me. I've been spending time with fools,
with lean assassins and the merely mean.
I check my shoes for scorpions each morning.

I had forgotten this sweet sting. A meeting,
coffee by the river with a well-grown man;
an ear for wit and nothing but the truth.

If I lean forward more than usual
in a brand new dress
we both know why.

If you take off your sweater
with a needless flourish
we both recognise the shape of you.

This afternoon I'll walk a different riverbank.
I wear you in my throat, my ankles, in my bones
for hours. It's nothing, everything; it counts.

First, cause no harm

I pay the bill, I leave a tip and when I turn
he's pulled that jacket on: sits on the table edge
so he can look me up and down as I walk back.
I'm shaking, as I'm meant to be.
He's practised this before, and not on me.

You have to laugh. You have to tug a forelock
at such skill; to render unto Caesar
what is due. I walk back slowly.
I have practised this before, and not on him.
It's an exchange of small lightnings;

an easy homecoming. We know the rules.
We wrote the rules, like everybody else
and as it goes, can no more step outside them
than a river can be still. We're in
and just now, laughing as we swim.

Fair play

Men, believe me. If in doubt, just
look her in the eye and say *I want to fuck you.*
It will work one time in three.

Miss out the games, transactions, tricks;
the leverage of compliments,
the calculations made while she is in the toilet.

Here's proof: one week of plainsong took this pair
from *I enjoyed the play* to the point
where clothes are an embarrassment.

They are giddy with getting away with it;
stiff and wet with words,
with the waterfall force of telling it like it is.

One time in three, it works.
The other two are lying.

February 21st

Not the first morning after but the second,
I notice wax-green crocus spikes beside the path.
Your house is sharp with sun.

Behind the car the drystone walls
are soft with moss, upholstering
the northern light into the lime.

Still warm with given touch, I slip the brake
and pull away across the Lyvennet's little bridge
into the uplands. The day is mine to claim.

A rook lifts from the white-green fell
blown and gladly battered, flailing with joy.
Your gate needs oiling, by the way. Even that, I like.

Shibboleth

I thought of girls who doodled yours in school books,
gasped it on the back seat of your first car;
had it inked onto their wrist and then burned off
or screamed it in the labour room.

You thought of those who murmured mine
in rented rooms, or grunted it in bikers' dens:
scrapped over it like mongrels with a bone,
intoned it as they got down on one knee.

And so we called each other Rochester and Jane
or Hot and Bothered; Desperate of Huddersfield;
and the tea-cosy names which keep love only warm –
hinny, honey, darling, baby doll –

until, today, you lean into the root of me
and speak the word I wear under my tongue,
that font-and-deathbed tag, my given name:
whispering the word that for a moment

stops the river, leaves me
naked on the bank in flames.

Your Helens and my Jonathans

After the kitchen table, sofa, stairwell and
(surprisingly) that photo booth in York,
we've made it to a bed. Just you and me
and everyone we've ever slept with.
Your Helens and my Jonathans; they stand
like hospice visitors around the bed
garlic-pale and probing, choked on spite,
exchanging notes and bellowing our faults.
We could eclipse them with a wink: so love,
turn on the lights and look me in the eye
and call me by my name. And when your tongue
makes me forget that syllable, I'll summon yours
until our ghosts are well and truly laid.
We'll honour them, but they must step aside.

Mowing

Blackbirds. Then machinery – and you, working
your flowered slice of Galloway above
the river. So, you trade ten minutes' birdsong
for a skim of spring-fresh sweat, a view of
water laying weedy ribbons in its path,
a weave of cut grass in the hopper. Then
a rest, in garden chairs. This easy aftermath;
an hour of stained glass tulips, two zipped lines
of contrail. Slow guitars, and heat and wine.
It's easy mowing but they've forecast rain.
I'm up for taking you to bed again
to clench in sunlit mischief, till you bend
to say *It's only six: there's time for that.
Let's lie down on the grass. It's early yet.*

Worship

Though the whole point of the visit was to see
the squat twin churches of St Peter and St Andrew –
neighbourly as housewives at a lunchtime fence,
respecters of a long-held boundary –

I don't recall which one this was. The tombstones,
brass and daffodils, the bulrush-ended bell ropes,
the hassocks with their lambs and lions
would be common to them both.

The font may have been Saxon, Jacobean, beastchain
clinging to its ochre stains. Our interest was elsewhere.
All I can say is that its granite lip was cold
and took a curve well; smooth against my buttocks

as I balanced on it, ready at hip-height
and took you in, least admirable lover,
in steady blasphemy. Hinged on need
we laughed ourselves to standstill at the chimes

and leaned against the sun-boned vestry door,
waited for the dust to settle on the altar.

Whales

At the bathroom door we bump into each other slowly
and take rest. It's two o'clock. The skylight makes us dim.
Your great frame drifts to mine. A noise of pleasure.

Naked, out of bed and both surprised to find ourselves
standing at all, we lean together. These are clearer waters
than the day can offer us. I touch my hardship, mute

against the only shape that helps. Your face, sleep-gentle
takes its ease in breathing deeply, rests on my warm hair.
Each body wants the other's foil and form, the shelter,

anything. You take my hand and toddle us to bed.
You spin once on your axis: heavy, looking for the deeps.
My longbones feel their weight. I reach to rub

that great dark skull of troubles. Wherever we go
we float untrammelled and extravagantly slow.
In the night, we wake up singing.

The End

The conversation's over.
I'm by the Thames today.
The river thick with ferries;
London shifting shape, as usual.
Latticed cranes turn carefully.
On the scaffolding a figure,
one fist raised against the skyline.

Remember *Zulu?*
That warriored horizon
when the victors raise their assegais
and chant a deep salute?
The singing's over, and the soldiers
are still dead in the stockade;
but it's a gesture, all the same.

A diet rich in birdsong

Don't get me wrong. The people are alright. The pubs
are much the same as ours inside. Apart from that
it's hard, this ease. The fields are rich as leather,
hedged and ploughed. There's sod-all in between –

maybe a Georgian brick and thatch affair, a coach house
here and there but no real villages – or where there are,
the houses stand like strangers at a bar. The vicarage,
the manor, strong and blithe, expecting sun.

Their trees are scarce but grand. They have no hills
but slopes that you could draw with one curved line.
Their soil is wide and warm, their weather large. I grant
the birdsong makes a blossom of your bones:

the lanes pile up with it, it falls like wanted rain. For all that
there is no *outdoors*; the land comes to the eye unasked.
Behind these high red walls are gardens, pear trees.
I'm ravenous for limestone. I am coming home.

Rooks over Avebury

There must have been a score of them;
all lift-and-dip-and-fluster, beak and feather
against half-formed clouds, greybonnet winds.

The circled stones lay under them unnoticed,
and none of our paths relevant to their high view.
They flew, it seemed, without direction. But they flew.

Begin

You forget how fast it happens, how little say you have in it –
two glasses of house white, a sunny street and you are ready for it
both, together, nearliness is swilling round the decks of Saturday,
love gets you in the forearms mostly, in the little hairs,
the tides of your own blood refreshed and quickly current at his voice,
the slope of muscle, the just-before of it. You barely know the shape
    of him
and not at all by touch but here's a gathering, a swell –
well bring it on, the crest of appetite, the breakers' shock and gift,
the force which only works if you can swim with it
oh here it is! the catch and shift of everything, the giddy spin
like fish in millions flicking into silver at a sound which only they
    can hear,
like seas heard from a hotel window as the day breaks briny;
seagulls crying everything awake again.

Society of Friends

If I hoped the silence here would answer
it did not. I sat amongst them and I wept.

An hour, we breathed together. I felt dizzy
and unhelped. There was a little coughing;

every now and then a slow breath, in or out.
The woman in the purple jacket stood and said –

Since Mary died I have been thinking
about grace. The loss of love is very sad.
I have been thinking that in anguish,
we experience grace; we find it
in the love of other people round us.

She sat. There were wild flowers
on the table in a pewter mug.

I cannot say that I was healed.
I knew, though, what she meant.

Kith

A word made scant by frequent use.
I like it for its urgency and spit, for its
necessity. I like it for its oldness,
for its slingshot certainty.

I like it for its plainness; for belonging
to the Northern tongue behind my teeth.
I like it for its fighting talk.
The known. The tribe.

Something I can recognise:
something that recognises me.
I am not who I think I am
but who you know me to be.

I will lift up mine eyes to the hills

We make our own winters. *Take the valley*
or the ridge, depending on conditions says the book.
The hills are locked in snow and I will walk
from Mam Tor, shivering, to Barker Bank.

The views are clear and treacherous, the sky
an unstoppable blue. Either road, the land
will carry me unnoticed, as the river bears a boat.
I'll walk the ridge today. I'll take my kite.

Acknowledgements

Thanks for support, inspiration and deflation to my writing kith: the Ann Atkinson Writers, Jill Abram, Jenn Ashworth, Alan Buckley, Jane Commane, Josephine Corcoran, Jonathan Davidson, Ian Duhig, Norman Hadley, Tania Hershman, Angi Holden, Sarah Jasmon, Michael Laskey (from whose exercise grew the title and concept of this book), Matt Merritt, David Morley, Hilda Sheehan, Anthony Thwaite and Tony Walsh. Thanks to the Poetry Society and to the Canal and River Trust, in particular Judith Palmer, Tim Eastop and Ed Fox, for supporting me so solidly as Canal Laureate. For late night conversations, wisdom and creative chemistry that fed directly in to some of these poems: Alastair Cook, Paul McVeigh, Kevin Reid, Simon Thirsk.

For the use of the wonderful cottage which allowed me to finish the draft of this book – the Hosking Houses Trust and the Stratford upon Avon Poetry Festival.

Thanks to my boating kith and to the actual crew who make possible my life afloat, in all senses: have a good road. There are too many others to thank by name, but thank you. Thanks above all to my pole stars Ailsa Holland and Heather Duncan (whose art appears on the cover of this book) and their families, who are always stumbling over me in the kitchen. See more of Heather's art at heatherduncan.co.uk.

Several of the poems in this book came out of an unpublished project with Martin Malone, without whom they would not exist. Versions of some poems have been published in the anthologies *Bliss* (Templar 2012), *Birdbook 2* (Sidekick, 2013), *Bang Said the Gun* (Burning Eye, 2013), *The Penguin Book of Sex Poetry* (2014) *Vanguard #21, Live Canon 2014* and in the following journals or blogs: *And Other Poems, Acumen, Angle, B O D Y, Cake, The Clearing, Iota, the Frogmore Papers, Magma, Paris Lit Up, Nutshells and Nuggets, Rialto, Spontaneity, the Telegraph magazine* and the *Morning Star's Well Versed* column. One or two appeared in the later editions of *Navigation*. *The Icicle Garden* won the Charles Causley competition 2013; *Infallible*, the Manchester Cathedral Prize 2014; *Begin*, third place in the Bridport prize 2014; *Whales*, second in the Wigtown poetry competition 2014; *A Nightingale for Gilbert White*, second in the Café Writers Competition 2014; *Like love* was longlisted for the National Poetry Prize 2014.

The first line of *No Seafarer* is the opening line of Old English poem *The Seafarer*. The phrase "We could eclipse them with a wink" in *Your Helens and My Jonathans* is of course from Donne's supremely earthy *The Sunne Rising*. The title of *from here on up all paths are informal* is lifted from a psychogeographical map of Portree by J Maizlish – see jmaizlish.com.

Keep up to date with Jo Bell's work and new projects at jobell.org.uk or @Jo_Bell.

You can hear poems from this book, read by Jo Bell, here: www.soundcloud.com/jo_bell